Marriage
vs.
Living Together
10 Reasons to Take the Plunge!

NATASHA BENEVIDES

ISBN-10: 1482070448
ISBN-13: 978-1482070446

DEDICATION

This one's for you Mom

with much love and a few chuckles

CONTENTS

ACKNOWLEDGMENTS

JC – I couldn't have done it without You

A special thanks to my collective sounding board:
Joel, Melody, Chenoa, Darren, and Shirley L

INTRODUCTION

This is a book that embraces the messiness of being an imperfect couple borne of imperfect people living in an imperfect world.

Lest I come across to you reader as a superior being who deigned to step down from her pedestal in the hallowed halls of perfect marriages and educate the unwed masses on how *I* think they should run their relationships, here's a brief and honest glimpse into my soap-opera-worthy life.

My parents never married. I wasn't married to my first child's father. I eloped with my first of two husbands when I was seventeen, and lived with my current husband for four years before we got married.

I could go on (and will later)...but this book is intended to offer a practical perspective on committed relationships, not be an epic saga with movie rights.

Given this history, why would I argue the case for marriage?

Because my choices might have been different if someone who had already navigated the maddening maze of modern day relationships – and lived to tell about it – shared some insight as to what was waiting on the other side.

Join me my friend, as we unravel the mystery of why marriage is and always will be better than living together.

REASON # 1
POP GOES THE QUESTION

"Faith is taking the first step when you don't see the whole staircase." – Martin Luther King Jr.

The day I proposed to my husband Joel was like any other day. We were holed up in our basement watching some random program on television. In all likelihood it was hockey, and I hadn't quite come to the realization that this sport was firmly established as a third party in our relationship.

It was a weeknight and we were both tired from work, the commute and the inevitable chores awaiting us at home. I looked at him through bleary eyes for a minute, feeling a surge of affection and contentment.

Suddenly I blurted "why don't we get married?" He tilted his head, chuckled, and then returned his attention to the game.

I found myself sitting up a little bit straighter. More awake than I'd felt all day. "I'm serious. I love you and I want to spend the rest of my life with you. Will you marry me?"

For another minute we sat in silence, staring at

each other.   He clearly couldn't believe I'd just proposed and frankly neither could I.

A deep longing that was holed up in a little dark room way in the pit of my stomach had just made an appearance.

A longing that wasn't satisfied with the few years we'd been living together. A longing that, no matter how far down I pushed it…*after all I was a modern, independent woman*…kept popping up like a moody jack-in-the-box.

I wanted to belong. To belong to someone and something greater than myself. I wanted that sense of truly being a couple. Not a 'right now' couple, but a lifetime couple.

Sure I knew like everyone else that the divorce rate was ridiculous and some couples who were together for decades wound up constantly bickering like two frenzied women fighting over the last pair of pantyhose in the sale bin, but this knowledge didn't matter a lick. The want was deep and real and would not be denied.

So we sat in stunned silence, my future husband and I. At last he said (in a rather obvious effort to stall for more time) "I'm the guy, shouldn't I be proposing to you?"

Apparently my sub-conscious mind had already plotted this whole thing out while I was sleeping because my immediate response was "don't worry, you can still buy me a ring." *Ha!*

"So…will you marry me?"

He started laughing but his smile had traces of terror at the edges. I'd made no indication prior to this flash proposal that I was anything but content living together. If he said yes, this would be a second marriage for us both.

Considering that the first marriages obviously didn't work out for either of us, his reluctance was understandable. I, on the other hand, was ready to jump in and give it another go.

"Yes sweetie, I'll marry you," he responded at last.

Therein lies the first vital difference between living together and marriage. It's *a* question vs. THE question.

Typically, living together just sort of happens. First it's a toothbrush, then a drawer, and then you're sharing the rent. Pooling your resources. It's a shoulder shrug agreement – "Why not? Makes sense to me." – as opposed to an official declaration of intent.

In no uncertain terms, a marriage proposal is a statement of love, devotion and the deepest level of commitment one adult can make to another.

Regardless of the struggles on the road ahead, a proposal says "I'm all in, no matter what."

REASON # 2
STAKE THAT CLAIM!

"My most brilliant achievement was persuading my wife to marry me." – Winston Churchill

"I don't see a ring on that finger!" At some point over the years, whether it be from friends, in a movie or elsewhere, you've likely heard this quote or some version thereof.

Picture it. The woman has hinted to her man that she's longing to hear wedding bells. He doesn't take the bait.

Frustrated, she goes out with her girlfriends to let off some steam and a cute guy starts making eye-contact. One of her friends, the trouble-maker, tells her to go ahead and flirt. After all... there's no ring on her finger. No ring, no claim. That's the rule.

A man stops for a coffee and the place is crowded. The only seat left is at a table occupied by an attractive young woman who, unbeknownst to him, is looking for her next relationship. He's invited to take a seat and she discreetly checks out his ring finger. No ring, not taken. That's the rule.

What's that you say? Some people work with their hands or dangerous machinery and don't wear their wedding band? Good point. In some marriages only the woman wears a wedding ring? Another valid observation.

Consider this. During a conversation with an interested party the question will inevitably arise as to whether you're single, with someone, or married. With marriage the commitment is clear.

When a person has a boyfriend, girlfriend or – the more current term these days – partner, what level of commitment would you assume they're at? Monogamous? Living together? Out of braces?

The truth is you don't know unless you specifically ask or they offer up the information. When someone's partner is either 'husband' or 'wife', there is no question as to the depth of their relationship.

If couples are living together but unmarried, there is a perception of wiggle room. Of potential availability should something better come along.

So is that to say marriages don't face the same challenge if one or both of the spouses are discontent? The commonality of affairs, sexual temptation, separation and divorce certainly debunks that myth.

Truthfully, if a spouse is not fully committed to the relationship and willing to work through the bumpy patches as lifetime couples do, an affair or other painful circumstance may develop.

However, the common view 'out there' is that there are different degrees of wrong when it comes to a married person cheating versus someone who is living with his or her partner.

Matt and Helen had worked together for just over a year. During this time their department head often teamed them up to prepare presentations for clients. Matt enjoyed working with Helen and had grown to admire her. She was pretty, smart and never tried to steal the spotlight.

One week a particularly challenging assignment was handed to them. They were on a tight deadline and worked through dinner several nights in a row. During these meals, they began sharing personal stories.

Afterwards Matt, a single, good-looking man in his early thirties, found himself thinking about her more and more. He began sending her funny texts and bringing in little treats each morning.

It wasn't long before Matt and Helen's working partnership turned into an affair.

Despite Helen's guilt and anguish over their relationship, Matt didn't actually view it as an affair.

He knew she was living with some guy named Jake, but so what? If her boyfriend didn't have the chops to stake his claim, then as far as Matt was concerned Helen was fair game. Once Jake was out of the picture, he'd get a ring on her finger right quick.

Stacey knew it was against the rules to fraternize with gym members. As a staff person, flirting could get her fired. The problem was Tony. Three days a week he walked into the gym, and her life, with rippling muscles and a smile like a ray of sunshine.

He would always take a minute to greet the staff and make small talk.

It was through these brief exchanges that Stacey learned Tony was in a committed, cohabitating relationship. Committed, but not married.

Which meant there was still a chance for her.

Stacey figured that if the woman he was with wasn't good enough to marry, it was only a matter of time before an opportunity would open up to show him what she had to offer.

No matter what modern society tells you we're still old fashioned at heart. If you're not married, on some level you're considered available.

REASON # 3
THE SHORT ARM OF THE LAW

"In law it is good policy to never plead what you need not, lest you oblige yourself to prove what you can not."
– Abraham Lincoln

"We don't need a piece of paper. In the eyes of the law, we're married." Huh.

Do you ever exceed the speed limit? Question or criticize authority? Take a pen, sticky note or paper clip from work? If you've answered "no" to all three questions, than kudos to you and your fellow brethren from the planet Mars.

On Earth, we humans – even the more conscientious of us – may unintentionally bend a rule or two now and then. Speeding happens to be one of my particular challenges. For some inexplicable reason I tend to view the speed limit as more of a suggestion than an actual law to be obeyed.

Now don't think for one second that I'm encouraging anyone out there to buck the law. Laws matter and we should always strive to obey them. This is an honest book. And honestly speaking, we're human and occasionally foolish.

Yet couples living together will almost always answer the question "so when are you two going to make it official?" with the old (and I do mean *old*...cohabitating couples have been using this line for decades!) "we don't need a piece of paper" routine.

You know what? If you're afraid of the evil marriage monster that takes a perfectly good relationship and destroys it before your eyes that's okay. Perhaps you've witnessed some marriages amongst your family or friends end in a train wreck.

Roberta still remembered the fallout from her parents' marriage. She was an only child and, for as long as she could remember, the volume in the house was always set at 'yell'. Her mother would pounce on her father as soon as he got home from work and natter at him about every little thing until he exploded in a rage and she wound up in tears.

Then one day daddy didn't come home from work. Roberta and her mom moved into a small apartment. At first he would come to pick her up once a week and take her out for dinner or a walk around the mall. These were special times for Roberta, he made her feel like a princess.

One week, he couldn't make it. And then another. As her dad faded out of the picture, her mom and the depression she was suffering from came into sharper focus. She barely spoke, the television constantly blared, and she was eating all the time.

At twelve years old, Roberta often found herself cleaning the apartment, nagging her mother to shower and was embarrassed to bring her friends home. At this tender age Roberta vowed that she would never get married.

Now a grown woman, she was true to her word. On the surface living with Ted seemed to be working, but a part of her always wondered if she had just taken the easy way out.

Deep down she found herself longing to be married, but was paralyzed by images of its ultimate failure.

Joe ran his contracting company like a well-oiled machine. He'd built it from the ground up and had a staff of twelve hand-picked employees. During his down time he played basketball with some of the guys in his neighborhood and faithfully visited his parents for Sunday night dinners.

His favorite activity though was spending time with his girlfriend, Alicia.

Having happily dated for two years, he'd recently been receiving signals from Alicia that she was hoping for a marriage proposal.

This was a game-changer for Joe and he was concerned. Sure he wanted to settle down and have kids eventually, but one of his buddies had recently gone through a nasty divorce.

He'd shared with Joe that his ex-wife was a

sweetheart when they were seeing each other, but once they got married it was like she transformed into a person he didn't even recognize.

Not only that, but when they went through the divorce she got half their assets and he *still* had to pay her monthly alimony support!

Joe owned his own house and his business was moderately successful. The thought that Alicia would be entitled to half if not more of what he'd worked so hard to achieve was horrifying.

When he expressed his concerns to a trusted friend, Joe was told that in the eyes of the law he could actually have Alicia move in with him for up to a year before she was legally considered his common-law partner – which meant she'd have no claim to his assets during that time.

Joe loved Alicia but was shaken by his divorced friend's experience. By living together instead of getting married, he figured he could always end things before the one year mark if she turned into some unrecognizable shrew.

So how can people like Roberta and Joe let their guard down when they've witnessed the failure and fallout of a marriage? It's called taking a calculated risk.

On various reality shows, contestants are expected to do ludicrously dangerous stunts. But before being sent out over a three hundred foot drop or into a car which is then lit on fire, they are equipped.

It's the same thing with marriage. There are many tools and resources out there to prepare you for what to expect, how to communicate well even with the tough stuff, and what really goes on after happily ever after.

Just because some marriages fail does NOT mean yours will. And if you have already experienced failure in a previous marriage, don't give up…get equipped!

Fear can be overcome with courage, willingness and wisdom.

REASON # 4
WHO YOU CALLIN' A COW?

"How can a woman expect to be happy with a man who insists on treating her as if she were a perfectly normal human being?" – Oscar Wilde

Back in the day people saved themselves sexually for marriage.

Especially women, who were considered impure if they were with a partner prior their husband. There was a common belief that if a woman gave herself to a man sexually before marriage, he would have no reason to marry her.

This belief was encapsulated in the popular cliché "why buy the cow if you can get the milk for free?"

That's foolish, you might think. Hmmm…let's do the math.

Over the past fifty years women have become increasingly active sexually and saving yourself until you're married is now considered borderline bizarre by mainstream society.

Conversely, according to a report study by the

National Marriage Project from the University of Virginia[1], over the same time period the stats for cohabitating couples have increased fifteen-fold while marriages have continued to steadily decline.

Is it really a coincidence that as women become more liberated men become less committal? Again I remind you reader that I am most assuredly not some high and mighty superior female who saved herself for marriage. I'm sad to say far from it.

For a long time I considered sex a source of power. I was desirable, in control, and could pick and choose as I liked. Later on I discovered two things that drastically changed my perspective.

First, did you know that for every mature egg we women produce monthly men produce sperm in the hundreds of millions[2]? *Hundreds of millions* in a single month!

Frankly with that kind of biological pressure on them, I'm surprised men aren't aroused by the site of a paper bag! And I thought I had power?? Pah!

Second, every time I engaged in this act without a deep, lasting and abiding love, a little piece of my soul fluttered out the window.

So women become more sexually active outside of marriage and marriage rates drop. Does that mean the only real point of marriage is to be monogamous and pop out a kid or two?

If that's the case why not live together? You're

in love. You're committed to this one partner sexually. Sounds fine right?

In an ideal marriage - which is *not* an impossible pipe dream but something that can be achieved through a healthy perspective, realistic tools and deep commitment to our partner - you are monogamous mates...*for life*.

This means that you can take your time to discover one another physically in a safe and loving environment.

You can have fun and explore and know that this person is devoted to you even when you go through the inevitable intimacy cycles of being active and fizzling...being active and fizzling...

I challenge you to search yourselves. Even when your ideal view of living together has been achieved, can you say with complete assurance that this is your sexual mate...*for life*?

That even when you hit dry spells (and if you think that won't happen now and then watch out!) neither of you will start to scope out greener pastures?

If the thought of having one mate for life makes you shudder, the truth is you're not ready for a long-term commitment.

Or if the idea of being with this *particular* partner for the rest of your days is what gives you the willies, it's time to face the fact that you're not right for each other.

In either case, playing house together is not a healthy situation for you or your partner.

SOURCES

1.   "Social Indicators of Marital Health & Well-Being." University of Virginia National Marriage Project / Institute for American Values. December 2010
http://stateofourunions.org/2010/si-cohabitation.php

2.   A Note to My Readers: though the several online sites I researched regarding egg vs. sperm counts were reputable, there were too many "tee hee" bloggers and enhancement ads for me to subject you to. Feel free to verify my mathematics as you deem necessary.

REASON # 5
YOUR FROG IS A FROG

"When a man opens a car door for his wife, it's either a new car or a new wife." – Prince Philip

Soulmates. Lifemates. The One. I confess to you reader that I'm a sucker for chick flicks and happily ever afters.

And then the movie ends and the waft of my husband just coming in after spending two hours fixing the lawn mower hits my nostrils. This is no manly scent from a romance novel. This is a flat out mixture of sweat, grass and gasoline.

Plus it's Saturday. The last time he shaved was Thursday and his cheeks look like I could use them to scrub the bathtub with.

Not that I'm exactly any great shakes either. Knowing it was chore day, I'm in a ratty pair of sweatpants and the top I'm wearing has so many old stains I can't remember its original color.

At this point (and it's about 2pm) I'm pretty sure I haven't brushed my teeth yet…dragons would be hard-pressed to outdo the odor of my breath.

During the time we lived together before our wedding nuptials, the appearance of my unkempt man with his occasional grumps and smells would cause me to wonder about an exit strategy. Undoubtedly my fluctuating moods and weight cycles had caused him to have a thought or two of his own in this regard.

Not in the beginning though.

When we first started dating he was my handsome hero. Everything he said was witty and profound. Any scents that came as a result of physical labor were simply a sign that he was a man's man. Just looking at him would give me a thrill and I was one of the happiest, luckiest women in the world. After all, against all odds, I had found my soulmate.

And because we longed to spend every possible moment with each other, we began living together.

It didn't take long before he was comparing my cooking to his mother's, making observations about my housekeeping skills, offering advice on what I should say and how I should act without my asking for it, and venting about his day like he worked in the pit of a volcano under prison guards rather than a regular office with regular people.

What had happened to my prince? My soulmate? The one that had been uniquely created just for me?

Yet again, it looked like I had been duped. Tricked. How sad that this was going to be just another failed relationship. But then I began to look on the bright side…*at least I hadn't married the guy.*

Once reality sets in and our heads are no longer in hormone land, we start to see the less pleasant traits of our partner.

When you're living together that deep and abiding commitment you made starts to feel a little less abiding when it's the fifth… twelfth…twentieth time you've argued about whether it's a man's right in his own home to leave the toilet seat up.

Whether married or living together, we all go through those inevitable moments when we wonder if we've made a mistake.

The difference?

Tolerance. When you enter into those vows for life, you come to realize that you may have to face fifty years of strewn about socks and hair in the drain.

The only way to thrive and survive with one another over the long haul is to increase your tolerance level.

Why? Because marriage is an investment that may experience a dip after the initial return but will abound again with very fruitful long-term gains.

This was certainly true for us. Once we were married our ability to accept one another in our 'froggy forms' increased significantly. Yes Joel has his flaws and I have mine, but those pesky peccadillos are just part of the unique make-up of our particular marriage.

Face it ladies, your frog is a frog who will likely make embarrassing noises and exude weird smells at inappropriate times.

And men? Your princess will age, gain weight and have moods.

With the time, love and depth of marriage our frogs do become Kings and we silly little princesses grow into our rightful role as Queens.

REASON # 6
THE WORLD ACCORDING TO JUNIOR

"It is easier to build strong children than repair broken men." – Frederick Douglass

In case you believe that children are not affected by whether or not their parents are married, allow me to share my personal experience.

My two oldest siblings were a result of my mother's first marriage. My third oldest sibling a result of her second marriage. As for this baby girl, I was the result of her brief and fiery cohabitation with my father.

Even though I know my mom loves us four kids and raised us as best she could while being a single working parent, I always had a sense of inferiority in comparison to my brother and sisters. After all, their fathers had really wanted to be with our mommy and them.

How did I know this when all the daddies were gone by the time I was old enough to reason? Because at some point they stood before an altar and declared their intent to be real husbands.

I didn't even fit in with the increasing group of kids at school whose parents were divorced. At least divorce was definable. Imagine that. The kids with divorced parents looked down on me with pity.

Why? In the hierarchy of children – and in case you've blotted out your childhood memories like so many of us these days there *is* one - being with parents who just live together positions you fairly low on the social ladder.

And if your parents lived together and then split up without even *needing* a divorce, my friend you are officially on the bottom rung.

As a child the concept of living together is really rather vague. No matter how the parents try to explain it away, the truth is as children of cohabitating couples grow and witness the 'real' families around them, it can cause identity issues that will plague them right into adulthood.

I need look no further than my own family. Although we are a loving and fairly close knit clan, relationship patterns were passed down as surely as big earlobes and a crooked baby toe.

Generation one (from 1960s forward):
- Two family members had a total of three cohabitating relationships

Generation two (from 1980s forward):
- Four family members had a total of eleven cohabitating relationships

Generation three (from 2002 to date):
* Four family members had a total of eight cohabitating relationships

Generation four (from 2011 to date):
* Still in diapers... outcome pending

Did you do the math? I did. If we had all been married during these times instead of living with our respective partners, it would have tallied up to a total of twenty-two marriages between us!

For those of you who believe that living together first is the gateway to making your marriage stronger, permit me to enlighten you. Of the above noted relationships only five resulted in marriage.

And of those five marriages only *two* are still standing. Statistically speaking, that's a *nine percent* success rate.

At this stage, you might be raising an eyebrow and wondering how I could possibly have any claim to making a case for marriage or helping you on your journey and I don't blame you.

Nevertheless, this is the stark reality of just one modern day family that has inherited 'relationship genetics' as a result of decisions made by the generations before them.

As you well know reader by either your own family history or that of others you're acquainted with, my family's fractured background is far from unique.

At its best marriage offers children stability and a sense of belonging to something bigger than themselves. Can living together really do that?

My daughters were in their teens when my husband and I married. At that point in their lives I expected our nuptials to have little or no effect on them. He was not their father and they were already young women with an eye to their futures.

Plus they had already been living under the same roof with my husband and I while we wrestled through the process of cohabitation.

That our marriage had an incredible impact on them was made evident right after the wedding ceremony.

Our oldest daughter, then eighteen, stood up and gave a speech in which she unexpectedly declared now that Joel and I were married, she would start to call him "dad"!

And my youngest daughter was grinning so hard for so many hours it seemed like her face would eventually split in two! Their joy astounded me.

To a kid (even the older ones) the act of marriage counts in a way that fancy explanations never will.

REASON # 7
FAMILY MATTERS

"Each person must live their life as a model for others."
– Rosa Parks

As indicated in the previous chapter, the day I married my husband was the day he became a father to my children. But he also become an uncle, brother and son.

While Joel and I were living together my family grew very fond of him. The problem was I had a fickle nature and history of destructive relationship patterns.

In truth, they simply didn't know if my lurking drama queen would rear her ugly head and I would call it quits in a fit of pique.

Their collective sigh of relief when we married was almost audible.

If you are in a committed, long-term relationship, at some point on one or both sides your family will be brought into the mix. Even if you have family members who accept your living together status, they can never be fully integrated because the connection is unofficial.

Ivan was playing basketball with his buddies when a text chirped from his phone. It was his partner Cassandra asking him to pick up her niece Katie from dance class as she was running late at work.

Even though they'd been living together for two years, he felt weird about her request. After all Katie wasn't *his* niece and it would be strange if he went to get her on his own.

Bethany adored her brother Tim's girlfriend Rachel. They had the same taste in shoes and quirky sense of humor, but Bethany was afraid of getting too close.

She knew her brother was loyal to Rachel and now they even lived together. The problem was Rachel wasn't the first woman Tim had lived with. Bethany had made friends with his past girlfriends, only to have them suddenly yanked out of her life when he got restless again.

Living together is a focus on you the couple, whereas marriage is a union for the entire family to celebrate and partake in. It is a cornerstone for others, a safe place for them to look to when the stormy seas of their own messy situations seem out of control.

The foundation of marriage goes well beyond the couple, and even the kids. It can have a tremendous and lasting impact on the extended family.

REASON # 8
WOULD YOU LIKE FRIES WITH THAT?

"I'm not a real movie star. I've still got the same wife
I started out with twenty-eight years ago."
– Will Rogers

Let's face it, we live in a disposable world moving at breakneck speed. Devices and technology become redundant almost as soon as you buy them. Movies, even blockbusters, hit the theaters and are gone again by the time you've paid for your popcorn.

Everyone is in a megarush to get nowhere fast and relationships are no different. We get swept up in the moment of someone new, speed into physical intimacy, scurry to move in together and zoom off again to find the next one the minute this one seems like it just isn't working.

Julie was thrilled that things were going so well with Mark. They'd been together for a few months and it was absolutely amazing. Her girlfriends warned that it was too soon after Ian and she appreciated their concern. After all she and Mark started dating only a week after her split with Ian, but who was she to stand in the way of fate?

The only problem was Julie still lived with her parents and Mark had a roommate. Spending alone time together was difficult. It seemed like they would never find a solution.

Then unexpectedly, Mark's roommate moved out. Julie moved in right away and things seemed great...for a week or so. But Julie hadn't realized it was Mark's roommate who did all the cleaning and most of the cooking.

They began fighting within a month and Julie couldn't believe what a mistake she'd made.

As it happened, she ran into Mark's old roommate Daniel at a bookstore one afternoon and they got to talking. Julie enjoyed their brief time together and they agreed to meet again for a coffee. Daniel was such a sweetheart. Now if only she knew what to do about Mark...

Round and round it goes. Unfortunately, unlike forever updating our technology – which depletes our money, or constantly eating take out – which depletes our health, the continual turnover of relationships depletes something far more serious – our humanity.

There's a flip side to the fast pace of our world. That old expression "they don't make 'em like they used to" applies. The majority of products and consumables aren't made with the same amount of care and quality they once were. They weren't made to last. As consumers we accept this and move on to the next product or upgrade as fast as our credit limit permits.

Like forgetting to wipe our muddy feet before going inside, this consumer mentality is carried right on in to the arena of relationships. If our 'purchase' isn't everything we expected or we come across a willing upgrade, we may find ourselves suddenly feeling stuck.

Living together is like having that money back guarantee tucked away in a mental mind drawer...*just in case*.

With marriage, we are given the opportunity to allow this lifetime relationship to unfold in due season and build something that, to our delight, is in fact made to last.

REASON # 9
A REAL SHOCKER

"People, even more than things, have to be restored, renewed, revived, reclaimed and redeemed; never throw anyone out." – Audrey Hepburn

So, how's that immortality working for you? Have you made the necessary arrangements to genetically alter your body so it doesn't break down, get creaky, grow old and ultimately betray you? *What's that?* You don't have to worry about that for practically decades still? Right, gotcha.

And what about that pesky work thing? Have you received a lifetime contract from your boss yet guaranteeing that you'll not only have a job forever, but if the company goes under they'll keep paying you anyway until you're good and ready to retire? Better get on that.

Hey what's happening with that electric shock collar? You know the one that zaps your partner when he or she sneaks a peek at something inappropriate? Did you get all the bugs worked out yet? Don't forget the remote control now.

Health concerns. Job loss. Temptation. These are just a few of the major issues every long term couple *will* face over the years.

If our day-to-day flaws are irritating to our partner, imagine the reaction when heavy stuff crops up.

Scott was saying something but Penny couldn't hear him. Her mind was still reeling from the sight that greeted her when she came into the room. Scott, her faithful, loyal Scott, transfixed by pornographic images on their computer. The same computer where she video-chatted with her mother!

"…don't know what came over me I just…" she tuned him out again. How could she even compete with these women? And why would she want to? Clearly Scott was not the man she'd thought he was. She always suspected there was something going on.

"...need help…can't stop…" Can't stop? How lame. Why was she still standing here anyway? They'd lived together for almost four years, with Scott repeatedly claiming they didn't need to get married as he was completely devoted to her.

"Don't waste your breath Scott. It's over." And with that, it was. Penny didn't give a second thought to his plea for help. As far as she was concerned he was only saying these things because he got caught, so good riddance.

Penny's reaction is certainly understandable but the fallout of her decision had a tremendous impact on them both. She found herself embittered toward men and went through a string of relationships where she would set out to destroy them before they started. The reason? To prove her point - that men were untrustworthy and she was better off alone.

Scott unfortunately lost the groundedness of a stable relationship. As with drugs or gambling, he had an addiction and needed help. He reasoned that Penny was right to leave. He was slime for doing what he did. Even so, with her gone his moral boundaries eroded and he delved further into his sexual addiction, wound up losing his job, and was arrested twice for solicitation.

Truly who can blame Penny for her quick dash to the emergency exit? They were only living together after all. Would she have been so hasty to break up if they were married?

Join me reader, as we travel back in time...

Edna smiled fondly at the flushed-faced boy on her knee. He'd just hopped onto the porch after running around the front yard shrieking delightedly while disrupting the leaves his grandfather Eddie kept patiently raking and re-raking into neat piles. He was three and a joy to both of them.

Being a grandparent held a special kind of happiness all its own and Edna was grateful for it. As Eddie looked over and waved, Edna felt a warm fondness for her husband of thirty-eight years.

Their daughter Amy was beside her, sipping an

iced tea. "Mom, I really hope that Paul and I are as happy as you and Dad one day. I don't know how you do it."

Edna continued to smile, but there was a hint of sadness in her eyes as she remembered a less than pleasant phase in their marriage before Amy and her brother were born. A phase that went on for five miserable years.

Five years of drunken nights, pleading, arguing and living on little more than peanut butter and stale crackers because what meager earnings they had were spent on booze. And look at them now. Their house paid off, their children settled down, and a beautiful grandson to shower with love.

She again glanced over at her husband, so very grateful that he'd stood by her back then as she battled alcoholism. Now with the bad news about his prostate, it was her turn to be strong for Eddie.

"The secret," she croaked to her daughter, "is weathering the storms."

When those shocking moments strike we need time to process, work through it and, if necessary, heal. Even us marrieds have periods when we wonder where the escape hatch went. The difference is we're less inclined to bolt when something bad hits.

Digging in and working through the storms of life together – even when one of you is the perpetrator – results in a new depth that cannot be achieved without that lifetime perspective.

REASON # 10
YES, I *SO* WENT THERE!

"Above all, love each other deeply, because love covers a multitude of sins." – The Bible, 1 Peter 4:8

Thank you reader for journeying with me thus far. We've had some fun along the way and it has admittedly been humbling but necessary to share with you a bit of my own less than stellar history.

Hopefully this book has given you some things to think about and you feel less alone out there!

Now I ask your indulgence as I offer you the tenth and final reason why being married is better than living together – the spiritual connection.

That fondness for chick flicks I mentioned earlier was borne from endless hours of having the television as my babysitter growing up while my mom was at work and my older siblings were in the throes of adolescence.

One of my favorite shows was "The Love Boat".

For those of you who don't know it, the show was a weekly comedy / romance about people finding 'the one' or realizing their current spouse was 'the one' all along. The antics were predictable and silly, but to a seven year old girl the writers were practically *brilliant*.

At that age it was never about the clothes, the innuendos or the one-liners, it was about the magical connection that happened to every couple or couple-to-be who set foot on that mystical ship.

Granted in the real world that ship would have barnacles and we'd get sunburned, but I've never been able to shake that belief in something magical, beautiful and pure about marriage. To me there has always been an inexplicable depth to this bond.

From the beginning I've offered you a brief glimpse into my patchy past with its destructive patterns. So what changed? What was *sooo* different about my relationship with Joel once we got married?

It went from being a relationship to being a union. From two people co-existing to a singular creation. A new entity all its own. Suddenly a faith I had been wrestling with, unworthy vixen that I was, blossomed in front of my disbelieving eyes.

From that blossoming, that foundation of faith, our relationship grew, our daughters flourished, opportunities opened up and our physical and emotional intimacy deepened.

This is what I know to be true in my own life. When I looked up and called out, God answered and my soul was never the same again.

Whether you are a person of faith or not sure where you stand on the subject, of one thing I'm positive my new friend – though you are most certainly *not* perfect, you most certainly *are* worthy of receiving that lifetime commitment called marriage and the wonderful adventure that goes along with it.

Please don't ever settle for less!

DON'T MISS THE NEXT VOLUME
IN NATASHA BENEVIDES'
KICKSTARTING COUPLES™ SERIES
...COMING SOON!

Made in the USA
Lexington, KY
24 April 2019